Simple Words of Praise

Amie W. Evans

INTRODUCTION

I am writing of my experience, along with the many other writers around the world, sharing the good news of how amazing, awesome, and sovereign our God is. He gives peace in the midst of the storm. He can keep you with a song or praise in your heart, a word of prayer on your lips, and a thank you ringing in your soul. I found this out many, many years ago, when I, was troubled or confused about any of life situations. God would give me great consolation through **simply words of praise.** I hope and pray that as you read these words, you will be blessed with much comfort and peace and that, your inner man will be encouraged and strengthen to continue from day to day.

Our God has the way and the words we all need to draw us closer to Him. John 14:1 states 'Let not your heart be troubled: Ye believe in God, believe also in me.' As you read these *Simply Words of Praise*, I hope your passion and love for our Lord and Savior Jesus Christ increases and your knowledge and realization that 'you can do all things through Him, as He strengthen and keep you'(Philippians 4:13).

I found out that He will speak to all of us that truly love Him and want Him to be our spiritual guide. 'To all of us who hunger and thirst after His righteousness' (Matthew 5:6). It might be through a poem, a song, a prayer, a sermon or any act of charity that you extend to your fellowman. Our God uses us in many different ways. I pray that as you read these poems and the inspirational phrases that God has given to me, you will be more determined to continue your Christian journey running this race with joy. 2nd Corinthians 7:4 states "I am exceeding joyful in all our tribulation.'

To know the things God has promised to us we must study His Holy Word (2nd Timothy 2:15) then you will be able to meditate both night and day, rightly diving the word of truth. When we know what to pray for and how to pray, there will be no wondering or guessing about the things you can have with His Blessing (all gifts are not from God). Let us read, pray, and meditate on His word and patiently wait on Him to answer.

Your Sister in Christ, Ms. Amie

Preface

After mediating on what Jesus means to me, I realized how I can commune with Him, anywhere day or night, at work or just enjoying the day. You can see His loving hand leading and guiding you if you would only let Him. When you are perplexed, confused, and troubled on every side, He will whisper in your spirit the thought that you need to bring peace, love, joy, and patience to your soul. 'He will equip you in what you need to operate in the fruit of His spirit' (Galatians 5:22). He is the one to call on to have that heavy weight lifted off of you. James 4:2 states that 'ye fight and war, yet ye have not, because ye ask not.' This scripture is plainly telling us we can fight these attacks, both feelings and emotions, if we would surrender them to the Lord of Host (smile, I have to tell myself this all the time). He will give you that perfect peace if you keep your mind staying on Him. Ask Him to deliver you from the spirit which has you so bounded.

As you read this book, I hope you can understand how I felt when my Lord and savior Jesus Christ put these **simple words of praise** in my mind and spirit. How His words flowed so sweetly to me, releasing a calm, peaceful, loving spirit. His words are like a strong medicine or anesthesia to soothe your mind.

Please remember what He has done for me, He can do for you, as you read, (Selah) meditate on each these **simple words of praise** and I pray that you will be enlightened and uplifted.

Your sister in Christ, Ms. Amie

Table of Contents

Inspirational Readings

The Bible

As I think of the Bible and what it means to me, it is truly the inspired word of God, I realize without the Bible, God's Holy Book we could not learn of His Goodness, about His Death, His Resurrection, and His Eternal Salvation, the Bible tells us what to do to be saved and how to stay that way. The greatest love stories, the greatest war stories, the great warriors and the kings, are revealed in the Words of God.

The Bible

The Bible is the Holy Book
That the Lord inspired
He choose twelve men to spread the word,
As, they, cross the countryside.

In the Bible, the words are great
Oh, what stories it tell.
You learn of Peter, of what he did
And of Jonah, in the whale.

The story of Joseph, it's in the Bible
For everyone to read
It tells of his coat of colors
And how he was sold to thieves.

The story of the baby Moses,
Of how his life was saved one day
Then you will learn, how God used him
To lead the Israelites away.

There are many other stories
That tell about the King,
How He died on the cross
That all mankind would not be lost.

My Soul

The Bible reveals man is made with three parts: Spirit, Soul, and Body. 1 Thessalonians 5:23 says '...and God of peace Himself sanctify you wholly, and may your spirit and body be preserved complete.' Webster's Dictionary defines soul as "the spiritual part of a person that is believed to give life to the body," and in many religions the soul is believed to live forever–a person's deeply felt moral and emotional nature and the ability of a person to feel kindness and sympathy for others, to appreciate beauty and art.

My Soul

My Soul cry's out to thee
Thou Lamb of Calvary
Carry me safely through as I go
Lord, feed me until I want no more.

My hands I raise to praise your name
Lord help me never more to change
Giving my life to you is my prayer
Your love to others I will share.
My Soul yearns for you to be my guide
Taking away all my hurt, pain and pride
Keep me, Jesus close to thee
Heaven is the place that I long to be.

Then my Soul will live for an eternity
Where joy and peace will never cease
The Angels and Saints will always sing
Glory, Glory to the King.

Jesus

Isaiah 9:6-7 states 'His name shall be called Wonderful, Counsellor, The mighty God, The Everlasting Father, The Prince of Peace, of the increase of His government and peace there shall be no end.'

J-- Is for Justify where all our sins are forgiven

E-- Is for Everlasting Life that our God will give

S--Is for Security in Him you can depend

U-- Is for United in one God we will trust.

S-- Is for save what you will be, because Jesus Christ gives us liberty.

Jesus Christ, is the only hope of this world.

The Book of Psalms

In the King James Bible there are 66 books, we all have our most favorite to read and study, all Praises and Thanks to God, for the great kings, disciples, apostle, prophets and the many courageous, faithful men and women that were chosen by God, to teach and inspire Christians on how we must live. *Psalms* a most powerful book, where there are scriptures to cover all of our emotions such as joy, anger, peacefulness, frustration, despair, happiness and anxiety. There are also prayers (see Psalms 35), for when you are afraid, as was David, when he wrote Psalms 2; are you frustrated by injustice read Psalms 79, Psalms 19, and Psalms 104. Celebrate the incredible power of God as it is revealed in His creation.

Psalms

Through David, God gave us the Psalms
A Holy Book to carry on
When it's strength you need
In Psalms you will find
The scriptures needed to heal the mind.

The Lord is my Shepherd
The twenty third Psalms
God gave to us,
To keep us from harm

Trust in God, never fret
In the book of Psalms
All of your needs will be met.

Saul (Paul)

Paul was actually born Saul. He was born in Tarsus in Cilicia around 58 AD in a province in the southeastern corner of modern day Tersous (now referred to as Turkey). He was of Benjamite lineage and Hebrew ancestry. His parents were Pharisees, fervent Jewish nationalists who adhered strictly to the law of Moses (who sought to protect their children from contamination from the Gentiles anything Greek was despised in Saul's household). Saul of Tarsus was a religious terrorist.

Acts 8:3 states 'He begin ravaging the church, entering house after house, and dragging off men and women, he would put them in prison.'

Saul was on the Damascus Road
All the Christians he swore to kill
He had an encounter with Jesus that day
That changed the way he would feel.

His eyes were blinded, he saw no one
But he knew that the Master was real.
God changed his heart he had a new start.
No more Christians he would kill.

His name was changed to Paul that day
The great apostle that we all know
A servant after God's own heart
Who taught Jews and Gentiles that they must pray.

Noah

In a world taken over by evil, violence, and corruption, Noah was a righteous man. He was the only follower of God left on earth. The Bible says he was blameless among the people of his time. He walked with God, being in a society saturated with sin and rebellion. Noah was the only man alive that pleased God. Over and over again we read accounts in Noah's life that he did everything just as God commanded in his life of 950 years, exemplified obedience since the wickedness of man had covered the earth like a flood. God decided to start over again with Noah and his family. Given very specific instructions, the Lord told Noah to build an ark in preparation for a catastrophic flood.

Hebrews 11:7 states 'after they entered the ark, rain fell on the earth for a period of forty days and nights. The waters flooded the earth for a hundred and fifty days.'

Noah

To Noah a servant of God
The earth is the Lord's
The fullness there of
All creatures great and small.

Before the flood
God gave Noah the plan.
To save his family
And start a new clan.

Noah, gather the animals
Two of each kind
Place them in an ark
Made from God's special design.

They were all locked in
As the rains begin,
Raining, forty days and nights
For them there was no end in sight

They sailed away
To safety that day
All other living creatures
Had a debt that they must pay.

Noah, and all in the ark was saved
To our God, He had prayed
With much praise in his heart
God gave Noah, a new earthly start.

Mary

As we keep living, we will have many ups and downs. I have found as I study God's Holy Word that there will be a story or parable to help strengthen and guide. I also found how important repentance is and how easy it can be to ask God's forgiveness for the things we have done or said that are wrong.

The birth of Jesus described in Matthew 1:18 states 'His mother, Mary, was engaged to be married to Joseph. But before the marriage took place, while she was still a virgin, she became pregnant through the power of the Holy Spirit.' (NLT Bible)

Mary the blessed virgin,
Choose by God, from above
To be the mother of Jesus
The Savior, the world must serve and love.

Mary, strong and courageous
Carried out the Master's plan
Her son Jesus, was born
To save the sinner man.

Mary, His Blessed mother
Her name, all Saints will proclaim.
With love and much honor
Her name will always reign.

Angels the Messengers

These are scriptures with Angels in them found in the KJV Bible.

'Be not forgetful to entertain strangers; for thereby some have entertained angels unawares.' (Hebrews 13:2).

'Bless the Lord ye his angels, that excel in strength, that do his commandments, hearkening unto the voice of his word.' (Psalms 103:20).

'And the angels, which kept not their first estate, but left their own habitation, he hath reserved in everlasting chains under darkness unto the judgement of the great day.' (Jude 1:6).

'When the son of man shall come in his glory and all the holy angels with him, then shall he sit upon the throne of his glory.' (Matthew 25:31).

'And he shall send his angels with a great sound of a trumpet, and they shall gather together his elect from the four winds, from one end of heaven to the other.' (Matthew 24:31).

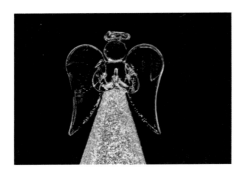

Angels

Angels are Guardians and messengers of a supreme being. Their existence is not supported by any scientific, evidence. Angels are biblical humanoid creatures; they are depicted as being powerful. Catholic Encyclopedic states Angels are represented throughout the Bible as a body of spiritual beings. They are intermediate between God and men. What are Angels? An Angel is a pure spirit, created by God. The Angel Gabriel is a messenger from God in three major religions: announcer of the Savior in Christianity, transmitter of scriptures in Islam, and interpreter of visions in Judaism.

Angels are spiritual beings.
They serve the Master's will.
They are selected by the Savior.
Oh what a story to tell.

Their spirit is all around us,
Keeping us safe and calm.
Another protection God provides
To keep us from Satan's harm

Angels watch over us
God, let them our prayers receive
Our burdens are always lifted
When they carry out our needs.

Angels are mighty warriors,
Which God dispenses with love.
They surround and protect the saints,
Whose names are written above.

Baptism
Our Lord Jesus, so divine
He gave us baptism as a true sign
The Lord Jesus was baptized by John,
To show us the way it should be done.

Under the blood you will go down
Arising with new faith
And wearing a new crown.
Father I stretch my hands to thee
Lord help me a new person to be.

Christian
Being a Christian is and honor
That you should explore
Your life will have meaning
More than ever before

Your thoughts will be gentle
Your actions will be kind
The Lord Jesus Christ
Will always be on your mind.

A Christian should be honest
And study God's plan
A Christian should always forgive
And love his fellowman.

Death

In the dictionary, death is defined as "the end of life, the total and permanent cessation of all vital functions of the organism." Death is an experience that raises many kinds of emotions in a person. The way we live our lives will speak for us. The wages of sin is death but the gift of God is eternal life, which ensures that if you live for Jesus Christ, you will live again.

When I think of Jesus' death, what it means for all mankind, the suffering, the humility, the love that He showed for us all, we must forever give Him the honor and all the praise. My earthly parents death will always be with me as anyone who has lost a love one knows but when I remember that Jesus' promise to die in Him, you will live again.

Death

When this life is over
And there will be no more
My sweet Savior, please meet me there
On your heavenly shore.

My soul will be at rest
No more races to run
Lord, please say to me
My servant well done.

Your face I hope to see.
In the clouds above
Lord, please grant me sweet peace
And your everlasting love.

When My Jesus Died

On the cross of cavalry
Where our Savior died
He bored our sins away
The day He was crucified.

He rose again the third day
The sins of the world were gone
He promise never to leave us
No, never to leave us alone.

The Holy Ghost the comforter
To you this day I will give.
For this is the only Holy Spirit
That will teach you how to live.

Jesus, your death shall not be in vain
As we hold up your Holy name.
Praising you Lord on high
As we wait to meet you in the sky.

Why Did He Do It?

Because He love all mankind
He came to earth to heal the sick and blind
He walked this earth like a mortal man
While holding the keys to the kingdom in His hand

He shared our grief and understood our pain
Knowing that some hearts would never change
His plan for you is that you would never die
When all your thanks and praise reach him on high

New grace and mercy He gives everyday
To all hearts that will repent and pray
You must live Holy to do His will
By studying His word, all truth will be reveal.

Life one day will cease to be
For God, has prepared an eternal home for you and me.

(from a sermon by Bishop Roscoe on 1/27/2013)

Resting Place

The grave is our final resting place
From all our worries and pain
We ask you Dear Savior
To meet us there, all our souls to claim.

Then beyond the grave
A better home is prepared
Angels singing songs of praise
And our sweet Savior, will be there.

Thank you Father for this new heavenly home
That comes beyond the grave,
For in you we found a resting place
Where we can forever give you the praise.

Prayers

'But when Ye pray use not vain repetition, as the heathen do for they think that they shall be heard for their much speaking.' (John 1:47).

Dr. Herbert Lockyer who wrote *Prayers of the Bible*, counted 650 prayers. He discovered 450 recorded answers in the Bible, from the prayers that he found. The word prayer is mentioned 128 times in KJV and 114 times in the Bible.

Prayer is simply communicating with God: talking and listening to Him. Believers can pray from the heart freely and in your own words. Learn to find prayers for your specific needs: Prayers for Peace, Prayers for Salvation, Prayers for Wisdom, Prayers of Repentance, Prayers for Spiritual Revival, Prayers for Children and Families, whatever you need, learn to take it to God in Prayer. The book of James 4th chapter states 'you have not, because you ask not.'

Mother's Prayer

My mother prayed
Both night and day
Asking God to show me the way
Her prayers have been answered
He's my King
He saved my soul,
I see the light
His Holy Ghost dwells
And His spirit redeems.
Thank you mothers for your Prayers
Thank you Jesus for you really cares.

Dedicated to my mother—Mayola Waters

Call Him

The day is over
Night is drawing near
Please sweet Jesus
My prayer to hear.
Guide us all across the life shore
Please open up the heavens door
Say to my heart Peace be still
Keep me Jesus in thou will.
When I stumble on my way
Ensure me Lord of and brighter day
Whisper sweetly to my soul
That, you will be with me, like days of old.
Remember Jesus, he will never change
His love for us will always be the same.

We must Pray

Our Lord and Savior Jesus,
He had to pray
Every knee must bow and every tongue confess
That Jesus Christ is Lord.
When we do this and truly believe
All of your spiritual needs will be met.

Create in Me

Have thine own way
Have thine own way
Lord keep me safe, each and every day.
Thou spirit Lord, please let abide
Keep me Lord by your side
Hold me Lord in your hand
Help me carry out your plan.

Create in me a heart of new
Teach me sweet Jesus, what I must do
Have thine own way
Have thine on way
Lord with my soul each and every day.

Be

Be - Be Holy for I am Holy

Be - Kind and strong

Be - Loving and Giving all the day long.

Be - Merciful and Just do no man wrong.

Be - Willing to serve, to help someone else.

Be - Wise as a serpent.

Be - Humble as a dove.

Be - Always willing to share God's love.

Be - Ready to work to carry out God's Holy plan
Having love and patience in your hand.

If these things you are willing to do. God almighty will be there for you.

Inspirational
Readings

Be at Peace

When I started working at my new job, at my desk this scripture is thumb tacked to the wall 'When a man ways are pleasing to the Lord, He makes even his enemies live at peace with him.' (Proverbs 16:7).

As I was reading this over and over, I focused on these words: 'He makes even his enemies live at peace with him.' What a blessed assurance we have that our Heavenly Father will make your enemies be at peace with you. Isaiah 26:3 states 'Thou wilt keep him in perfect peace whose mind is stayed on thee.' Lord we pray to keep our mind on you daily.

Lord we thank you for hand of protection, and for angels that are dispensed all around us guiding and leading us throughout the day.

'Blessed are the peacemakers: for they shall be called the children of God.' (Matthew 5:9).

'And the peace of God, which passeth all understanding shall keep your hearts and mind through Christ Jesus.' (Phillipians 4:7).

Let him eschew evil, and do good, let him seek peace and ensue it.' (1 Peter 3:11).

Peace

Lord, help me do your holy will
Spreading your peace and love to all mankind
Sharing with others how we must live
Letting them know that your love is divine.

Being a Witness

We were in Vacation Bible School at our church and our lesson was on how to be a witness for our Lord and Savior Jesus Christ. The question asked was how to lead someone else to Christ and how can we be a successful witness? Our witnessing must be controlled and lead by the power of the Holy Spirit, it was brought out in our studies that it is not what you say to someone but sometimes the way you react or speak to the situation.

Are you always complaining and never happy? Do you let everything add gloom and despair to your life? As a witness we should exemplify the fruit of the spirit according to Galatians 5:22-23 which states 'you must show love have compassion, peace, joy, meekness and longsuffering.' Jesus said 'And I, if I be lifted up from the earth, will draw all men unto me.' (John 12:32). Let us as believers examine ourselves to see what kind of a message we are sending to others.

I will tell the story
Of our Lord and King
I will tell the story
How His love redeems.

Jesus the True Vine

John 15:5 states 'I am the vine, you are the branches. If a man remains in me and I in him, he will bear much fruit; apart from me you can do nothing.' I was reading a resume from a lady and as I read her work experience, I truly felt that she had love and compassion for others. She had been a house mother for one year at a group home and at another home she had been a house mother for two years, and last but not least, she was responsible for training, transporting and scheduling young girls for meetings, classes and appointments that would help them to mature in their growth both spiritual and financial. John 15:5 let me know that she realized how mighty our God is. He is the true vine that holds us up and we are the branches that flow from His love as long as we stay connected to his vine He will hold, keep, protect and nourish us, our fruit will let us become effective witnesses that will display love, peace, and longsuffering which will draw men/women to Him.

ABUSE

Webster's Dictionary defines abuse as "to use wrongly, to mistreat." Ephesians 5:28-29 states 'So ought men to love their wives as their own bodies. He that loveth his wife loveth himself.' I worked the 3-11 shift at our local hospital on the Psychiatry Unit and this young man came to visit his wife who was the patient on my floor, you could see the pain in both of their faces, in her medical records it told of the many times abuse was displayed in their home. Abuse destroys self-confidence; it can destroy all moral values, and sometimes the person's desire to live. After feeling despair and sorrow, for them and their family, God, put these words in my spirit about abuse.

Abuse is a terrible thing
It inflicts grief and so much pain
Mothers and Fathers and all the Kids
Lose love and respect and have no pride.

They hide their hate, and feelings inside
They lose their purpose, and love no one
They can become violent and use the gun.

They need someone to understand
To take control and hold their hand
They lie to each other, oh what a waste
If they would only turn to Jesus, for His amazing grace.

Their problems would be settled
They would lose all grief and pain
When they turn to Jesus,
What a great victory they will claim.

If you are guilty, your family you abuse
Ask the Lord, to give you comfort
And your evil temper you will lose.

Having No Guile

'Jesus saw Nathanael coming to Him, and said of him, behold an Israelite indeed, in whom is no guile.' (John 1:47).

Webster defines guile as "insidious cunning in attaining a goal crafty or artful deception, trickery, fraud, deceit."

How wonderful it would be if Jesus could say this about you or me. There is no guile in my servant. His or her heart is pure, their love is sincere and their prayers are full of thanksgiving and praise to our Lord and Savior Jesus Christ.

Just like King David in Psalms 51:12-13 states 'Restore unto me the joy of thy salvation and uphold me with thy free spirit,' (13) 'Then will I teach transgressors thy ways, and sinners shall be converted unto thee. Lord we pray that all our ways be pleasing unto thee all the days of our lives.'

Heavenly Father please help us remember
Each day as we struggle
To do the things that are right
If we would yield Lord to thee
You will fight our fight.

Simple Words of Praise encouraging every heart that calls on the name of the Lord. In the Bible there are many different names given to the one True God, whatever name you Worship and Praise Him (Jesus, Yeshua, Adonai, El Shaddai) are any other Holy Name, always knowing that He will bring peace, hope and joy to your soul.

Contentment

My Sweet Savior, talk to me
He gives me Peace, Joy, and great Harmony
We must strive to do His will.
Keep His commandments as long as we live.
Salvation and Joy, He promised to us
As we keep our hearts full of His trust.
Don't delay give God a try
He will be with you when, it's your time to die.
Contentment and peace is yours to have
When in the Lord Jesus Christ you dwell.
So Christian friends do not despair
He will provide your every care.
In your hearts please say yes.
In my Sweet Savior you will have rest.

Through It All

When times are dark and clouds are gray
When the light is dim and there is no way
I will lift up my eyes unto the hills
Knowing that my Sweet Savior forever lives.
As saints of God, we know what to do
Stand steadfast and prayerful
God will always see you through.

Trust

As mountains are high
As skies are blue
The Lord God almighty
Will be there for you.
Call His name
Give Him the Praise,
He will be there all of your days.
Trust, Love, and Honor
And of course Obey.
Let our sweet Jesus will show you the way.
Just keep on trusting
In God's words for it is true
For God has already done.
What He said He would do.

My Mountain

Life is like climbing a mountain
You must be prepared for the climb
On the way up it will be rocky
You may get caught in the vine.

On this Christian journey
Many rocky roads you will face
You must have on Holy Armor
And Christ should be your breastplate.

When you stumble and fall
Get up, start a new climb
Christ will be at the top of your mountain
Your feet He strengthens in His love divine.

You may be bruised and full of scars
Your life seems filled with despair
Remember Christ is at the top of the mountain
To guide you to safety through your prayers.

You can smile when you reach the top
For it will not have been in vain
Stretch out your arms and then proclaim
There is Victory in Jesus name.

Burdens

Your burdens can be heavy
You will always be in despair
When you travel along in this world
And God is nowhere
You must let the Savior in to do His bless will
His will for you is salvation,
That's why He died on Calvary Hill.
Learn to read your Bible
Learn how to pray
Your prayers will be answered
And you will be saved that day.

Lord I Thank You

'...be thankful unto Him, and bless His name.' (Psalm 100:4).

'Give thanks to the Lord, for He is good: His love endures forever.' (Psalm 107:1).

After reading these scriptures, I understood why God put this poem in my spirit, we must express our gratitude and tell Him how thankful we are for everything large or small.

Lord, I Thank You

For the sun that shines during the day.

Lord, I Thank You

For the birds that sing and the butterflies at play.

Lord, I Thank You

For the rain that falls and nourish the trees.

Lord, I Thank You

For the rivers that flow and the fish in the seas.

Lord, I Thank You

For the wind that blows and gives us the breeze.

Lord, I Thank You

For the flowers in bloom, search a pretty array.

Lord, I Thank You

For these sweet miracles You give every day.

Hope

He has delivered us from such a deadly peril, and He will deliver us again. On Him we have set *our Hope* that He will continue to deliver us. (Paul, an apostle of Christ Jesus by the will of God. 2 Corinthians 1:10) Then there was Dr. Martin L. King, Jr.

Hope

Hope, is the start
Of facing things that are new.
It is the driving force,
That's needed to stimulate you.

Hope, is the substance,
That keeps you going strong
It drives you to do better
Then conquer the things that you long.

Hope, generate desire,
For a need to do what's right
It gives you the courage
To stand up and fight.

Hope, is the evidence
Of things that are unseen
We hope and pray to God, each day.
To fulfill all our needs and dreams.

Hope, for the future
Is to do God's Holy will
It should be your greatest priority
And should be your greatest thrill

Our People

In the month of February, the calendar lists it as Negro History month. February is when most African-Americans reflect on the past through radio programs, television shows, movies in the theatre, and sermons from the pulpit reflect on the lives of blacks placed in slavery and the injustices we have had to endure from then to the present. We, the born again believers, know that it was God who brought us this far and He will see us safely through.

2nd Chronicles 7:14 states 'if my people who are called by my name will humble themselves and pray and seek my face and turn from their wicked ways, then I will hear from heaven, and I will forgive their sin and will heal their land.'

Our People

A race of people that have withstood
Slavery, bigotry, from most mankind
A race of people, I am proud to say
That race of people are mine.

The Black race have weathered
Through the storm of time
For Jesus Christ
Controls our wills and minds.

We give Him the praise
For sustaining our race
He, let us continue
Through His amazing grace

From slavery whips and small huts
Cotton fields and corn we shuck
Pushing the plow, till the sun goes down
He, is the one, who turned things around.

He, held our heads up to the sky
Put pride in our lives
Then taught us why.

Me and My People

I did not know from whence I came
The things our forefathers had to endure
I was born in America, the land of the free
Only to realize that free is not free.

I am an American,
From an African descent
Our fore fathers were brought here
By much greed and pretense.

Chained and bound and sometimes whipped
As, they sailed the seas on the large slave ships
Afraid and scared of the things they must face
As, they sailed the seas, to this strange new place.

They were misused, beat and badly bruised
With nothing to call their own
From dusk to dawn they pulled and rowed
Until their hands and knuckles were deeply torn

Their pride was stripped
Much grief they had to bear
They banned together in languages unknown
As, they took it to their God in prayer.

Slavery has ended, but the fight goes on
There is still so much, more we must do
We have to love each other and help your brother
The way our Lord and Savior commands us too.

Traveling

You can see the Glory and the mighty hands of God in everything you do or in everywhere you go. Driving across the countryside from Alabama to Tennessee and seeing the mountains, clouds, and trees will let you witness just a little of God's provisions for us. Looking at all the marvelous sights which He has provided has brought peace and tranquility to me, I thank Him for that and for these words He gave to me.

Traveling

I love to travel
Across the countryside
Seeing all the beauty
That God provides.

The trees so strong and very tall
Green in the summer, red and yellow in the fall.
The grass, a pretty carpet of green
Supplying splendor to the scene.

The sky above a beautiful blue
So vast and large, it is always in view.
The clouds forming a different design
Floating above can soothe the mind.

The birds are flying
From tree to tree
Oh, what a beautiful sight to see.

Fields of corn that we pass
Fields of cotton how the memory last
Cows grazing on the hill
Let you know my God is real.

A Flower Bouquet

As the season's change and the trees and flowers start to bloom, you can witness how awesome God is. As you watch the flowers and gardens grow, remember 1 Corinthians 3:7 states 'So then neither the one who plants nor the one who waters is anything, but God who causes the growth.'

Dedicated to the memory of my husband Thomas and for my daughter Angelia, who God has blessed with a growing hand and a love for flowers.

A Flower Bouquet

You will cultivate the soil and
Water it each day
From this labor of love and God above
You will have a beautiful bouquet.

First you will see the stem
Then the tiny leaves
A little bud a blooming
As it sways with each new breeze.

As you pick each flower
To make up your bouquet
Think of the love and the miracle
That gave you that pretty array.

Time

I was watching a video on you tube by a young minister, an 18 year old evangelist named Kyle Deny. He was preaching a sermon titled *This is no time to waste time* and that is when I thought of this poem that my sweet Savior had given to me.

Time

The clock on the wall, is ticking away
The time is pasting fast
As we look back on our deeds
Only the things we do, for Christ will last

Lord, with each minute and precious hour
Our hearts, we pledge to you
Grant us your grace, let it continue each day
To help a lost soul in finding their way.

As the clock tick on, keep us we pray
Humble in our hearts everyday
With a steadfast mind staying on you
Where our love for you, will never stray.

Time to Jesus, we cannot measure
For a year is just a day
When our hearts get heavy, too hard to bear
That's the time for prayer sweet prayer.

With each minute and precious hour
Remove all our guilt and stain
Make us free to worship thee
Declaring all things, good in your Holy Name.

The symbol of the Lamp

'The spirit of a man is the lamp of the Lord, searching all the inner depths of his heart.' (Proverb 20:27).

Inward parts of the belly relates to our deepest feelings it is a reference to the origin of our thoughts and motivations.

The spirit being expressed in a person may be of God, or may have accepted strange fire, from the enemy of our souls. There is mystery of iniquity operating in the midst of great deception. (see more at 2 Thes. 2:7).

'Lo I am with you always even to the very close and consummation of the age.' (Matt. 28:2).

Psalms 2 tells us that King David, warns us about the end time and a new world order conspiracy against the covenant of the Messiah. David clearly saw the end time, apostasy, and the raging of nations against the legitimate blood righteous rule of the returning Messiah.

Apostasy—Great falling away.

Repent

You must repent
For the wrong you have done
Then you start anew.
Jesus, said I will forgive
My love I, will give to you.
Your life will be happier
Your joy will be complete
Your soul will be anchored
And nestle at the Savior's feet.
What peace and satisfaction
What a great honor, you can claim.
All because you repented
And called on Jesus name.

When the Trumpet Sounds

God, revealed His Holy Plan
So that all men could understand
That the wages of sin is death.
Only through Him, can you find Peace and Rest.

His Peace will dwell,
His Spirit will reign,
To all of the Saints,
To Him they will proclaim.

The Trumpet will sound
The Holy call will go out.
Only those whom God, have sealed,
Will be able to hear the Holy Shout.

Woe, Woe, Woe, the cry will be called.
The Bridegroom is coming for His Church today.
Woe, Woe, Woe to everyone,
There is no more time to Pray.

Let us prepare to meet the King.
Where Holy, Holy you will always sing.
Peace and happiness will fill the earth,
And there will be no more doubt, about the Savior's Birth.

(Revelation 20:10) and the devil that deceived them was cast into the lake of fire and brimstone, where the beast and the false prophet are, and shall be tormented day and night for ever and ever.(Revelation 20:15) and who so ever was not found written in the book of life was cast into the lake of fire.

The End of this book, but the story will not end.

Acknowledgement

All praise and honor to our most High and Supreme God. I thank Him for not giving up on me, how He continued to put words of inspiration and praise in my spirit; although I did nothing to nourish His gift. I thank God how my faith has increased, how John 14th chapter means so much to me (smile it could be a different story).

I want to thank my cousin Carol Pender for her encouragement and thank her for all the messages and uplifting greeting card that she send to encourage our family and others.

I'd like to acknowledge the anointed men of God that I have been a part of their leadership and spiritual guiding: Elder James Henderson at 11th Ave C.O.G.I.C (deceased), St. James Missionary Baptist Pastor Gerald Jones, and my now Pastor Bishop Demetrics Roscoe and Pastor Pauline Roscoe, Living Church Ministries International.

My niece Latasha Watters, how she labored and put everything in its proper order to make this work come together.

Your Sister in Christ, **Ms. Amie**

I would like to thank my aunt for giving me this opportunity to help her put her words into print. I've learned over the years that if you have something to say, it's best to write it down so it can be passed down from generation to generation which allows them to know what kind of person a relative was in the past. Helping my aunt put her book together was minimal on my end because everything flowed from her and I just happened to know how to use Word. I hope you find as much enjoyment from reading her poetry as I did from putting it all together.

Latasha

(this page intentionally left blank)

Made in the USA
Columbia, SC
13 September 2021

45405452R10035